NOTES TAKEN AT M

Notes taken at Meetings

with Maurice Nicoll

January 18, 1934 to April 28, 1934

EUREKA EDITIONS
UTRECHT – THE NETHERLANDS

by the same author

Dream Psychology

The New Man

The Mark

Living Time

Psychological Commentaries
on the Teaching of
Gurdjieff and Ouspensky

Selections from Meetings in 1953

Simple Explanation of Work Ideas

© Eureka Editions 1995
ISBN 978-90-72395-08-5

Foreword

In 1931 Dr.Maurice Nicoll received authority from P.D.Ouspensky to pass on the Ideas he had received from him and G.I.Gurdjieff. Maurice Nicoll devoted the last twenty years of his life to this task which culminated in the five-volume *Psychological Commentaries on the Teachings of Gurdjieff and Ouspensky* (Stuart 1952, reprinted by Shambhala in 1984, Weiser in 1998 and Eureka Editions in 2008).

This book contains random and fragmented notes of Maurice Nicoll's Thursday meetings held in London, between January 18 and April 28 in 1934, which were jotted down by a member of his group. I have felt that these were well worth putting into print because they give a very clear idea of the way in which these meetings were given while keeping purely to the Work Teaching.

This Teaching is oral and at this time there were no books about it, so if people missed a meeting or were unable to understand what was given, they may have had to wait years before the topic came up again.

Gurdjieff was aware that people would distort what he taught and Ouspensky reports on page 96 of *In Search of the Miraculous* that when Gurdjieff was asked if one could find "anything real in the teaching and rituals of existing religions, or anything that might lead one to attain something real", he replied:

"...Yes and no".... "Imagine that we are sitting here talking of religions and that the maid Masha hears our conversation. She, of course, understands it in her own way and she repeats what she has understood to the porter Ivan. The porter Ivan again understands it in his own way and he repeats what he has understood to the coachman Peter next door. The coachman Peter goes to the country and recounts in the village what the gentry talk about in town. Do you think what he recounts will at all resemble what we said? This is precisely the relation between existing religions and that which was their basis. You get teachings, traditions, prayers, rites, not at fifth but at twenty-fifth hand, and, of course, almost everything has been distorted beyond recognition and everything essential forgotten long ago."

The contents of this booklet are intended for people who have already studied the Work Ideas, so I have made no attempt to explain the terminology.

For further reading please refer to the bibliography at the end of this book.

The Editor

A NOTE ON THE AUTHOR

One of the leading British psychologists of his time, Maurice Nicoll was a student of Jung, Gurdjieff and Ouspensky. At Ouspensky's request, he devoted the last twenty years of his life to passing on the ideas he had received from his teachers. This devotion culminated in a five-volume work *Psychological Commentaries on the Teaching of G.I.Gurdjieff and P.D.Ouspensky**.

Dr.Maurice Nicoll was born in 1884 in Scotland, the son of Sir William Robertson Nicoll, the well-known littérateur. In his youth he met many famous men at the brilliant gatherings at his father's house in Hampstead, among whom were Lloyd George, Asquith, Sir James Barrie, the young Winston Churchill, and Lord Riddell who frequently refers to conversations at this home in his Diaries.

Dr.Nicoll took a first in Science at Caius College, Cambridge, afterwards qualifying in medicine at Bart's Hospital. After studying in Paris, Berlin and Vienna, he entered upon his career as a Harley Street specialist.

In World War I he was a captain in the R.A.M.C. and was in charge of a hospital in Gallipoli. He described his war experiences in a book, In Mesopotamia, published in London in 1917 under the pseudonym of "Martin Swayne".

In 1917 another book came from Dr.Nicoll. This was *Dream Psychology* and in it Dr.Nicoll acknowledged his

---

* The latest edition has an Index added.

profound debt to Dr.Jung with whom he had studied in Zürich.

On his return to Harley Street after the war of 1914-18 Dr.Nicoll joined the late Dr.George Riddoch at the Empire Hospital, where there were many famous men on the staff. He became a pioneer in psychological medicine and published many papers on medical psychology, from which William McDougall often quoted in his neuro-psychological volumes.

In 1922 Dr.Nicoll went for a year to the Institute for the Harmonious Development of Man which G.I.Gurdjieff had established at the Château du Prieuré, Fontaine-bleau. He had already met the Russian philosopher P.D. Ouspensky in 1921 who described the teachings and personality of Gurdjieff in the volume, *In Search of the Miraculous.* Up to 1940 Ouspensky lectured in London. In 1931 he authorised Dr.Nicoll to conduct groups for the study of the ideas of Gurdjieff which he continued to do until his death, also writing a five-volume commentary on the teaching of Gurdjieff and Ouspensky.

Dr.Nicoll's leisure activities included building, music, literature and the drama. He painted in oils and water-colour, and the water-colour illustrations in his early book, *In Mesopotamia*, were his own work.

About his teaching Dr.Nicoll said: "Just as we are to-day finding out about all sorts of chemicals, such as the sulphanilamides, penicillin, and streptomycin, so do we have to advance to the study of the poisons of the mind and the emotions, the outlines of which further develop-ment were laid down in the Gospels."

He also said: "The intention is to indicate that all teaching such as that contained in the Gospels, and many

8

teachings both old and new, in the short period of known history, is about transcending the violence which characterizes mankind's present level of being. It affirms the possibility of a development of another level of being surmounting violence."

He further said: "....as we cease to invent ourselves, so we cease to invent other people... we begin to feel a common existence which is without passion, and simply what it is, without further definition...."

Maurice Nicoll with daughter Jane
after his stay in Fontainebleau (in 1923)

WORK WORDS AND PHRASES

It is important to use them with intention and not let them become habitual. Dr.Nicoll once said "We must all watch this so that we give to each Work word its true meaning so that it is always fresh and full of intensity for us; to lose the freshness is a great loss because it means that we are sleeping or dozing and to doze when using a Work word or phrase is unpardonable, anything but that; doze if you must while using life words but not Work words."

NOTES TAKEN AT MEETINGS
from January 18, 1934 to April 18, 1934

January 18, 1934

In answer to the question "Do all impressions start an octave?"

Maurice Nicoll: No *impressions* start an *octave*. Man is incomplete, *man cannot do*. "If ye would be perfected" – (Not perfect). The top storey of the factory is in darkness, the second story is only partly lit up, the bottom storey is the only one fully lighted.

Self-Observation. Self-Remembering.

Maurice Nicoll: Why should we self-observe? Someone might ask this question who had been told this Work was a method. It makes one feel more *awake*.

If you can *observe yourself* while for instance you are identifying and at the same time *Self-Remember*, then something might be done. *Self-Observation* without *Self-Remembering* does not necessarily change anything.

Sensations are too complicated; take the thought: "It is unfair that I should have to work so hard and become so tired." If you can observe this thought and *Self-Remember*, the bodily tiredness will go on but you will be more free from it.

Try the exercise of saying to yourself "I wish to remember myself" in the midst of your activities for half an hour; you should be able to do it for three days. You will find that you do not wish to remember yourself at all; you wish all kinds of other things, for a cup of coffee, to look at yourself in the glass; very few of our wishes are not connected with appetites. We rarely wish for anything else. You don't wish to remember yourself, you will grow ashamed of this.

"I wish to remember myself". Every word should give a shock to the system. If you can make the chemical H 24 in yourself, everything becomes lighter. "I wish to remember myself"... It is like a signpost to China.

A greater emotion can drive out a lesser one. Some emotion connected with the work may drive out a smaller emotion. After a while all sorts of emotions connected with *The Work* get grouped together.

As children we are only *Essence*. *Essence* stops growing at about six. *Negative Emotion* comes to us from outside, from our parents, (taking this very broadly).

Personality grows around *Essence*; *Essence* grows from the ashes, from the death of *Personality*.

Personality becomes more rigid as we grow older. My greatest enemy is Dr.Nicoll, humming and hawing as if he made the world.

Self-Remembering can cure many things, make the machine more balanced, cure nervousness and physical things.

Identifying when one is worried does no good to anybody. The worst thing to do is to worry about anyone as you prevent them from helping themselves.

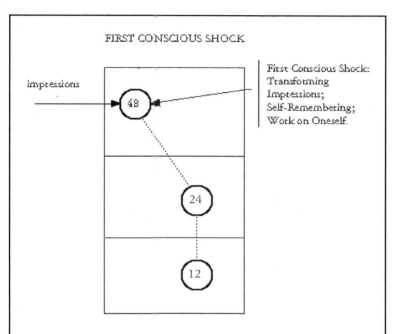

First Conscious Shock. This happens where Do 48 enters the upper storey of the "factory," where Hydrogen Mi 48 is present (from the beginning of the air octave.)

January 25, 1934

Maurice Nicoll: There are two types of man, ascending and descending; this is from Ouspensky's book [*A New Model of the Universe*], it is not the system but approved by it. Most people nowadays are of descending type. People of descending type must not be brought into *The Work* because nothing can help them. They must descend before they can ascend. It would be a waste of force for them to be brought into *The Work*.

Criminals are of descending type, forgers, embezzlers, murderers. A person who has been in prison is quite different from an ordinary person. It is very easy to descend. "What is the use of anything?" Take a few more drugs, get drunk.

As a doctor this theory of descending type has been of interest to me. I have come across people whom I tried to help and wondered why they could only be pushed up so far and then fall back. After ascending we must descend. Jacob saw angels ascending and descending the ladder, (though I believe that means something different). We hope we are of ascending type.

Some people are of stationary type. This explains prolific writers, they have done the same thing before and before, each time amplifying and doing it a little better, so that it is not quite the same. This explains writers like Dickens, who wrote such an enormous quantity of words with such ease. Statesmen are as a rule of stationary type.

According to Mr.Ouspensky, (but I can't accept this) descending man at last disintegrates. Before he reascends he must reach some nadir of misery.

Recurrence. After you have been in the work some

time you will say: "But I have so much to do with myself, how can one life suffice?" The idea of recurrence comes in here.

Time is Breath.

Cosmos below Man: Cosmos above Man:

	Molecules	Cells	Man	Organic Life	Planets	Sun
Impressions			1/10000 sec.	3 secs.	24 hrs.	80 yrs.
Breath		1/10000 sec.	3 secs.	24 hrs.	80 yrs.	
Day and Night		3 secs.	24 hrs.	80 yrs.	3 million yrs.	
Life	3 secs.	24 hrs.	80 yrs.	3 million yrs.		

Maurice Nicoll: A molecule lives for three seconds and then recurs. The sun sees our whole life as one. Man is a cell in organic life.

Study history from the point of view of the waking and sleeping of organic life taking 80 years, and make it interesting to yourself. It is interesting to me but why should I tell you?

We see nerves as lines, to a higher intelligence our lives are lines intersecting.

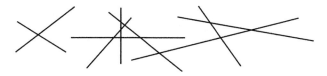

The nerve is not a line to itself.

Time

Maurice Nicoll: Everything is now. Jesus Christ – Julius Ceasar. We will go on sitting like this for ever unless we do something to change it. We are always dying and being born again, of just the same parents. It is no use shooting yourself, you can't shoot your own life. If you have ever maltreated anyone it is there. It is no use saying, "There, that's done, and thank God it is over. Anyhow I shall never see him again."

Question about getting rid of negative feeling.

Maurice Nicoll: What do you want? You cannot go on with this *Work* if you want to be negative. What carries you on is a feeling for work. What keeps the soldier on parade? (but no, that's fear, not love) There is the balance between yes and no. After a while a *conscience* is born in one in connection with the work which says, "Don't be negative", "Don't be the victim of imagination". I may know privately that I was negative last night, and in the morning be uncomfortable about it, not, you understand, because I have made a social fool of myself, by putting my elbows on the table, for instance.

17

This conscience acquired by education, such conscience is different for different countries, but the conscience connected with the work is not, this is *Real Conscience*.

February 1, 1934

Maurice Nicoll: There are divisions within oneself but they cannot be correlated.

	I	Nicoll (*False Personality*)
Essence		Personality
	I	IIIIIIIIIIIIIII (*many I's*)

There are degrees of mechanicalness. My way of walking is mechanical. That is right, it should be mechanical, up to a point. It would be very complicated to have to think about every step one took.

We have a facility in *lying*. We get bored. A child may get bored and play at being Queen of England all the afternoon, but this leaves a legacy behind. With girls it often begins with imagining oneself a princess. A boy may imagine himself an engine driver. The funny thing is that he may actually become an engine driver, and yet he will be driving that engine in imagination all the time, through the night and so on.

There is a good use for *imagination* but for a long time we must look at bad use. Nothing in man is useless and as he has imagination then that must be useful.

We have a facility in *lying*, like savages strutting about on the beach dressed up in beads etc.

A doctor may imagine himself healing thousands, or sitting in the proper attitude by the bedside of a child with pneumonia. But then what is best for the child is not foremost in his mind but his own picture of himself. He is not really considering the child.

Imagination builds up *False Personality* and gives one an organised picture of oneself which one carries about like an enormous Christmas tree in front of one. And everything hits on that instead of one's real self.

If *the Work* did nothing but rid one of one's *False Personality* it would have given one an immense gift. At first everything would seem flat and dull, but afterwards, if one could stand it, everything would be much more interesting.

It is nonsense to think that one could talk with masters (yes, masters) with this *False Personality* on one. In the schools anyone who wanted this Teaching was put for four years to be kitchen boy and kicked and knocked about, and heard nothing about the Teaching. If he could stand it probably he wanted the Teaching, and probably by that time he had not much *False Personality* left.

Question: Why should we try to Self-Remember?

Maurice Nicoll: Because the machine cannot be properly balanced, we cannot be in the state we should be in, without *Self-Remembering* and at times waking state during the day descends to dreams, but not quite to the dreams of sleeping state, there is a definite click when that is reached. And, if you can do it, there is also a quite definite click when consciousness begins.

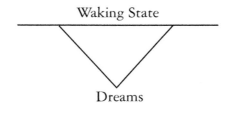

Waking State

Dreams

Why should we try to get above this filth, this dirt which is made by imagination?

Miss X: Because it is a lie.

Maurice Nicoll: Yes, that is a very good word for it. *Imagination*, ideals, are bad, because they are a form of self stimulation. A man goes to look for the ideal woman and does not see the actual woman at all. And the same the other way on. This causes a very great deal of sickness.

We must separate ourselves from the clamour and uproar going on within us all the time; we must see that it is not I. We must be able to see every thought and emotion passing in front of us and not only in difficult moments, but all the time.

If we try to *Self-Remember* and cannot, it is better to leave it for a time and try again later.

There is a parable, a fable, in *The Work*; Man is all the time on the edge of a precipice, with his back to it. If he looked down he would probably fall over. There is 'Help', but he must make a jump for the 'Rope', and then he will know what it is not to *Internally Consider*.

The imaginary world cannot mix with real life, any more than earth can mix with water. If we could stop the bad imaginary world then wars would stop.

We are in this bad state for various reasons, because we are on a very bad earth, because we are under the influence of many laws, and partly by *accident*.

Pictures must be bad for us because they make us ill; if we stopped having them our bodies would work quite differently, with different *hydrogens*. As it is we have to get on as best we may.

False Personality may be a sense of one's own importance, from position, something one's rather clever at, etc.

The difficulty about seeing one's *mechanicalness* is that people don't see their own way of being *mechanical*, their own "top hat", for a long time.

It would be quite right to say in this *Work* that Mr. X is angry, not meaning the real Mr. X at all.

There is a division into Nicoll and real self, not Dr. Nicoll and real self; the fact that I am a doctor may be connected with something quite real in me, though I may have all sorts of false ideas about myself as a doctor.

It is not only in one's *False Personality* that one can be hurt. *Essence* can be hurt by the loss of someone loved, or if one loves someone and something unfortunate happens. *Vanity* can be hurt, that is *False Personality*, *pride* is more from *Essence*. Big emotions touch *Essence* but we don't live with big emotions.

THE TWO TRIADS

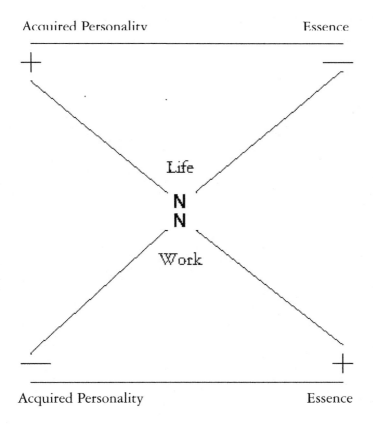

Acquired Personality   Essence

Acquired Personality   Essence

February 8, 1934

Chief Feature.

Miss X: What is *Chief Feature*?

Maurice Nicoll: Yes, I knew that question was going to be asked tonight. (Not by you of course) Better to leave it. *Chief Feature* (this is my private view and not *the Work*) is the relationship of *Essence* to *Personality*. It cannot be admirable though many people think it is. A gambler, for instance, will be a gambler in all he does. *Chief Feature*, generosity for instance, may be the very thing we have to work against, or miserliness, but it is really something more complicated than any of these.

Chief Feature is the deciding factor in all crises.

Aims.

It is better not to talk about *aims*, they are private, for yourself, they must not get mixed up with someone else and *False Personality*. If people ask you "What is your aim?", it is better to tell them something else.

I don't like talking about aims, they are private. But have an *aim* of some sort, however wrong and however inadequate, and you will find *the Work* will help you at once.

It is easy to start with *Moving Centre*, as the fakir does, to hold oneself in just such a position for a length of time. It is more difficult to start psychologically.

A man may decide that he eats too quickly. It may

be quite easy for him to eat more slowly, for another man it may be quite impossible because it may be connected with his whole emotional make up. He would have to start from his emotions, make aim from Emotional Centre.

Change.

Maurice Nicoll: One can change oneself but not the world. It is best to take it from the very broad point of view, we are on a very bad earth, under so many influences. There must be a certain amount of suffering in the world. People think that if there are these conscious people and they have power they can make things lighter, that if Christ appeared in the world He would make everything easier. That is not so.

Take disease. There must be a certain amount of disease in the world. If you find a cure for one you make another worse.

Imagination.

It is stupid to say, "That is only *imagination*", as though the *imagination* were nothing. It is very powerful.

Past.

One can luxuriate in regret for one's past because then one thinks one has paid in some way. *Imagination* comes in when one thinks of one's past. If one could really bear to see it and think what one ought not to have done in certain circumstances then when that particular thing comes again (in *recurrence*) one may act better. If one is more *conscious*, one cannot bear to look. If one is working **here and now** there may come flashes from the past connected with what one is now working on.

Think of yourself in connection with ill will, of all the harm you have ever done simply through ill will. It is unbearable to think of. One makes a litter of oneself, like making a mess in one's study and finding it there next morning.

Aim.

If one can make *aim*, the ship must be going somewhere, with a rudder and *The Work* immediatly helps one. It may be *aim* against petulance, irritability.

Life is a pit, and we can make a ladder out of this pit or it is a prison. Esotericism will help us make this ladder, that is what esotericism is for.

Mr.X: Is it right to have two aims going at once?

Maurice Nicoll: Yes, if you can remember them. You may get a picture of yourself as a person with two aims going on at once. Mr.Ouspensky was once talking to a man and asked him what his *aim* was. He said "Not to be negative under any circumstances whatever". Not a very modest aim.

This Work strikes at a man's *vanity. Man cannot do.*

False Personality.

Have you ever seen yourself making a fuss, that

is all from **False Personality**. A man may be so angry with you that he wants to kill you and that is from *False Personality*.

People who attack one another in the law courts, do so from *False Personality*, as a rule.

If you could really dislike yourself, your False Personality, something might be done. It is your greatest enemy. There is no change without changing it.

Fear.

You must not work from *fear* – that is illness – but from *understanding*. One gets connected with a certain source. If one turned to something else one would cut oneself off from that source. *Fear* crystallises the *negative parts* of *centres*, but you must submit to authority. You might refrain from talking about this *Work* from *fear*, that would be wrong. It should be from *understanding* why you should not talk about this *Work*.

It might be quite all right to fear that you are not working.

One must separate from *False Personality* and then there is a background of Real 'I'. (At a certain point the child separates from the outer world; "that is the table, this is I." The separation from *False Personality* is like that).

A quite definite stage is reached when work begins, and a long time elapses before it does. You may say of someone, 'he is good', but does he work?

Blame.

One must get rid of all idea of blame. I have heard this over and over again. Man is *mechanical* and therefore behaves like that.

Everything is discontinuous, there are blank periods, coloured and uncoloured emotions. It never occurs to us to work on blank periods.

There can be no work without suffering.

HEAVEN

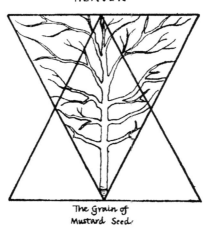

The Grain of
Mustard Seed.

EARTH

February 15, 1934

Mr.X: Is there any difference between right and wrong?

Maurice Nicoll: Well, if you want to go to Edinburgh is it right to go to Sussex? Right and wrong are relatives. But taking the ten commandments 'Thou shalt not steal', for instance, it is wrong to steal for many reasons. It gets you into difficulties but it means much more than that. You can steal other things besides money.

Then, is it wrong to be a gunman? Well, is it very different from all the rest of life?

We do not think enough about this, that we are not *awake*.

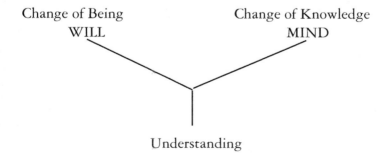

Waking

Sleep

In ordinary life *Being* is usually far behind *Knowledge*.

Change of Being   Change of Knowledge
WILL   MIND

Understanding

Being and *Knowledge* should be equally developed for balance.

Knowledge does not effect *Understanding* without the development of *Being*. What knowledge? Knowledge, that *we are asleep*, for instance. Usually in Western men, knowledge e.g. scientific knowledge, is far in advance of *Being*, therefore knowledge is used destructively.

Mr. X: What exactly is *Being*?

Maurice Nicoll: That is a good question, but exactly! Exactly, I don't know what *Being* is, but for example in certain circumstances a man always tells a lie, another man always tells the truth, that is *Being*.

Chief Feature.

It can be told in a novel but not in one paper. For example, a man's *Chief Feature* may be always to shift responsibility. How he did it in different ways in different circumstances could be told in a novel. *Chief Feature* is a twist in one; recognition of one's *Chief Feature* comes much later.

Maurice Nicoll: Well, let us talk about *Being*. There may be many levels and we are the lowest.

———
———
——— *Levels of Being.*
———
———

I may be at a point where no more knowledge will help me. Then I must change *Being*.

Question: How is it some people seem to grow better in their environment? Healthier, like healthy plants.

Maurice Nicoll: Why will you all bring it down to bodily health? It has something to do with that.

Remember the hydrogen table, food for man is H 768, not food for man is H 1536. Raw potatoes are not food for man. You can cut them up, pound them, they are still not food for man. But cook them, that is a *change of Being*, then they are food for man.

Mr. X: I might change my *Being* and my fellow men and women will not notice it?

Maurice Nicoll: It would be noticeable; you would not be angry where you were angry before and not depressed where you were depressed before.

We consist of *many different 'I's*. One will be hating someone at a particular moment, and you will hear yourself saying certain things then another 'I' will be loving them.

Sometimes we think we have changed *Being* when it is really the 'I' that has changed. Marching around waving flags changes the 'I'; so does a holiday change the 'I's.

There is a fable, a parable, in *The Work* that man is like a house full of servants and only one telephone. Sometimes one servant answers the telephone and sometimes another, and they all use the master's name, so confusion results.

There are *four ways of changing Being*:

> *Fakir Way*
> *Monk Way*
> *Yogi Way*
> *Fourth Way*

The *Monk Way* is not known now, at least there is no evidence of it, but formerly there were monasteries where the Teaching of Christ went on.

The *Yogi Way* is not possible for us, because we would have to go out to India and train for a long time and even then might not be admitted.

The *Fourth Way* is **here and now in daily life**, and we cannot do it if we bring ordinary ways of thinking of things into it. We must get sanction, permission, room, space to change. Where one man has gone and changed his *Being*, he makes room for another.

We must be able to observe which *centre* is being used. In reading for example, we usually read with *Moving Centre*, sometimes with *Emotional Centre*, rarely with *Intellectual Centre*.

Each *centre* has its own memory, *Moving Centre* has a very good memory. You learn to skate, for instance when you are ten, much later you begin to skate again and in a very short time you can do it.

There can be no *observation* without reference to *centres*. One must look where one does not want to look, where one usually does not look. One must find out what needs changing (not the things one usually thinks of, such as smoking, getting up late, eating too much).

If one puts the feeling of I into all the 'I's that come up they use all the force, there is nothing left for changing.

February 22, 1934

Miss X: Do all the 'I's come from mechanical use of *centres*?

Maurice Nicoll: Do you understand what different 'I's mean, because you should not ask questions theoretically. Well, let us talk about these *centres*. First of all we will divide each centre into halves, I will tell you why later. Then each centre has three parts; *Intellectual*, *Emotional* and *Moving* part of *Intellectual Centre*, of *Emotional Centre* and of *Moving Centre*. These are again sub-divided.

What would moving part of the moving part of the *Intellectual Centre* be? Talking – our ordinary mechanical talk – and emotional part of the moving part of *Intellectual Centre* – curiosities, little curiosities, what did he wear, what did she wear, what did he or she say? We use an enormous amount of force in these petty curiosities which might be used for change of *Being*, and we get involved in many things which do not really concern us, because we live under the law of accident and things which really have nothing to do with us affect us.

Intellectual part of moving part of *Intellectual Centre* has to do with little plans, like how to get from here to Oxford St.

The emotional part of moving part of *Intellectual Centre* (curiosity) in the big emotional part of *Intellectual Centre* would be love of knowledge.

Many people become really ill from incessant talking (moving part of moving part of Intellectual Centre).

The petty curiosity of emotional part of moving part of *Intellectual Centre* is a low kind of curiosity which involves us in difficulties.

Figure I – Intellectual Centre

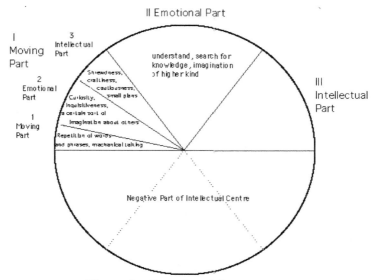

Figure II – Emotional Centre

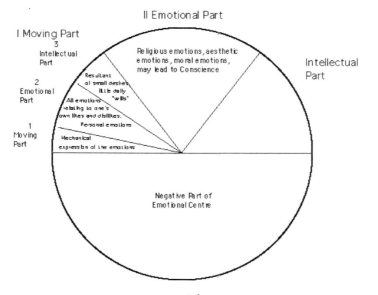

Figure III – Moving Centre

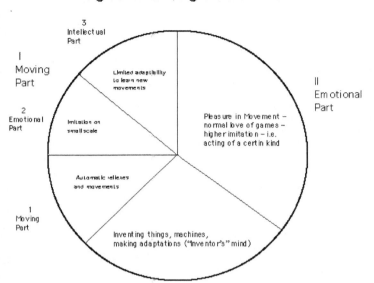

III Intellectual Part

The moving part of moving part of *Emotional Centre*. Facial expression of emotions, purely mechanical.

The emotional part of moving part of *Emotional Centre*, purely momentary likes and dislikes, which will take away much force.

Intellectual part of moving part of *Emotional Centre*, momentary wills. Larger 'I' in Emotional Centre would be aesthetic emotion, or religious emotion.

The emotional part of moving part of the *Moving Centre*, a low plane of imitation, for example if you have been to see a play or a film and some of it lives with you for an hour or a day or a week. If this is carried into the bigger emotional part of the *Moving Centre* and you can stand the training, it may be ability to really act. Transient imitation may be merely different 'I's coming up.

There is wrong working of centres because we are nearly all the time in moving parts of centres. It is as if we had quite a good house to live in, and lived all the time in the cellar; we may complain bitterly about the cellar, living in the cellar might make us ill, but we never think of moving into the rest of the house. We never seriously think of changing ourselves, we think of changing our circumstances, but we could change ourselves, and then circumstances might change as well.

Reference to observations of *centres* helps us in our observations.

The different 'I's are really in all *centres* at once.

We are in little 'I's all the time and we must gain knowledge of these, a different kind of knowledge than any we are used to.

If only we could get an intelligent *aim* then much might be effected. The little 'I's take our force, we are eaten by life. *Observing 'I'* must gather about it many other 'I's and much data.

Personality sends messages to *centres*, and to which centre it thinks it ought to go. *Personality* acts as secretary but has her own ideas about where messages should be sent. It is like: Red rag – Bull – Anger. Spot on carpet – personality – emotion.

Observing 'I' must observe what *Personality* is doing, and not put the feeling of 'I' into *Personality*.

After a time we may get a taste of all these little 'I's and dislike being in them, a very good stage to have reached.

Essence.

Maurice Nicoll: All *Essence* has the same hydrogen density. But *Essence* is different in different people. It is not a good thing not to have much *Personality*, because *Essence* can only grow through *Personality*. It is very interesting that *Essence* cannot grow by itself. It is very hard work to make *Personality* passive.

Essence grows, then a hard shell of *Personality* (imitation of parents etc.) grows around it. This shell causes much suffering in later life. We find ourselves doing and saying thing we do not really wish to say. Life would be much richer and fuller without it. It is easier at first to see different 'I's in other people. We take it for granted that we are a unity.

We must *observe* NOW, it is only in the **now** that we can change anything; I can only pick up this chalk now, not next week or last week. We are never in the present, always in the past or the future.

Depressed 'I's take on a depressed posture. By assuming a depressed posture, we may begin to feel depressed.

If we could remain in the same 'I' all day long there would be some unity; if this were a bad 'I', well that would be unfortunate.

We are very complicated machines.

Moving Centre is very clever. When we are learning to drive a car, at first we use *Intellectual Centre*, and that is very slow, then suddenly we can do it without thinking.

To help in observing try to go against something mechanical, something mechanical in bodily movement.

Suggest to me a polite 'I', a political 'I' with your

movements. When your dinner comes, Eating I is uppermost. These 'I's have memory but that is a very big question. 'I' are on the *Rolls* of *centres.*

Miss X: Is *Essence* in all centres?

Maurice Nicoll: *Essence* is centres, we are born with centres.

The Sun Octave

Sun	Do	12	Real I
All Planets	Si	24	Essence
	La		
Organic Life	Sol		Personality
	Fa		
Earth	Mi	48	Body
Moon	Re	96	False Personality

Suggested reading: *The Commentaries* page 1685 (written on 28 March 1953) : The Secretary and the three bosses.

[After this commentary was read Maurice Nicoll said the centre of mechanicalness is probably situated in the mid-brain. 99% of our life is purely mechanical.

We are in prison.]

March 1, 1934

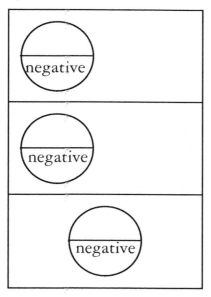

This *system* teaches that nothing we are born with is useless and our *Negative Emotions* are useless. We are not born with *Negative Emotions*. We acquire them, from our parents, from life. Every part of every *centre* has its uses, but *Negative Emotion* is useless, it can be got rid of.

Try *not expressing Negative Emotions* as an exercise for one day.

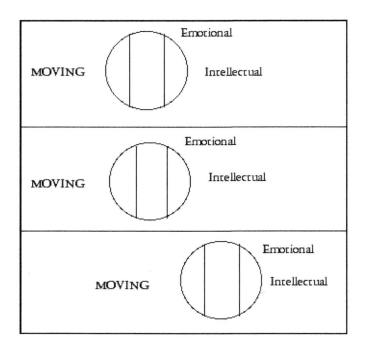

We live in *moving* parts of *centres*.

Negative Emotion is infectious. *Negative Emotion* gives us a sense of power because we can affect other people; when we say objectionable things we pass our *Negative Emotions* on to other people.

Our memory remembers all the bad points of someone we formerly liked and now dislike, and forgets all the good points. We forget how disgracefully we behaved.

Essence cannot grow while we are negative.

If you have something to do that you don't like to do, immediately you become negative. If you have something to do for someone you dislike, you do it badly.

If *Moving Centre* is working on something in which we are emotionally interested, one gets impressions from it, but in most work (factory work) there are no impressions.

Most literature, most poetry is negative.

Do not *identify*, do not hurry to look at an accident in the street to see how badly he or she is hurt. I was with an ambulance in a street once and every head was at every window. *Identifying*. The man who is always in a hurry, working against time, is *Identifying*. Then he has three or four hours when his work is finished and he has nothing to do. *Identifying* cannot be defined, there are many ways of *Identifying* which can be read in expression or gesture. **Later** there are conscious ways of expressing *Negative Emotions*.

In ordinary life if you feel negative towards someone you do not see them any more. You cannot do that in *The Work*, in *group work*. You must overcome the *Negative Emotion*. Some people think they have no *Negative Emotions*, when they really have them just like you or me, but they seem very little and unimportant. Others hide them under a gentle exterior and think they are nothing.

If you have to climb a hill and are tired, that does not make you negative, but if you climb it because I have told you to, that makes you negative towards me. Tiredness makes *Negative Emotion* but not fatigue. In fatigue, when you have walked 20 miles and tired yourself out, you are much less prone to be negative, because then *False Personality* is passive.

Negative Emotion makes unimportant things seem important.

45

If we are working at something and think we ought not to be, that makes *Emotional Centre* negative.

We live in little 'I's all the time. What is contradiction to little 'I's is unity to larger intellectual I. People who are always in little I's may be brought into *The Work* accidentally, but cannot remain in it.

The action of life on us makes negative states.

How to protect ourselves against the action of life:

1. Increase in *Self-Knowledge*, knowledge of our *Being*.
2. Trying to *Remember Oneself* (which creates separation).
3. Trying not to *Identify*, taking pleasure in negative things.
4. *Non-considering*.

Many people crystallize out in their *negative emotions*. I advise you to avoid such people.

There are three lines of work:

1. *Observation* of *Negative States* in oneself.
2. *Observation* of *Negative States* in other people. (That is no help at first.)
3. *Observation* of *Negative Emotions* in life.

We must try not to be negative about life.

TECHNIQUES FOR WORKING ON NEGATIVE EMOTIONS

(1) In outer parts of centre	(2) In middle parts	(3) Inner parts
Irritation	Resentment	Hatred
Impatience	Self-pity	Jealousy
Feeling of disappointment	Melancholy	Malice
Feeling hurt	Apathy	Envy
Small worries	Suspicion	Fear
Boredom - Indifference	Sulkiness	Resentment
Small envies	Rage	Depression
Indignation	Habitual worry	Sense of meaninglessness
		Despair
Dissatisfaction	Dislike	Violence
Embarrassment	Guilt	
Raising Objections	Nostalgia	
Try not to express it	*Self-Observation is needed - new thinking*	*Transformation only possible through prayer and Self-Remembering*

March 8, 1934

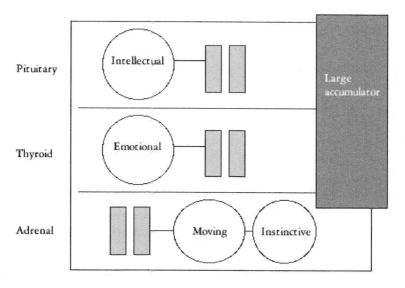

Pituitary

Thyroid

Adrenal

Intellectual

Emotional

Large accumulator

Moving   Instinctive

See also figure 42, page 233 *In Search of the Miraculous*

Pituitary, thyroid, adrenal, are not work terms.

Behind the *small accumulators* is the *large accumulator* which we never ordinarily touch. During the war, after enduring much and having no rest, all fatigue suddenly vanished and one went on quietly and calmly, having touched the *large accumulator*.

Each centre has the other accumulator which touches the big accumulator. The best way to rouse Intellectual Centre is to think.

We never are really tired, only by habit, by association. We think we have done a great deal when really we have done only a little.

49

Each *centre* has two accumulators connected with it. If *Instinctive Centre* acts through fear on the big accumulator, this gives energy to *Moving Centre* to make right movements. If *Instinctive Centre* acted on *Emotional Centre* instead of on *Moving Centre*, movement might be paralysed.

We can observe *Moving Centre*, in muscular movements.

Negative Emotion tenses, other emotion relaxes.

Ordinarily when we are negative we do not observe our movements.

We may *observe* that our hand is clenched but not have the force to relax it, just to be aware that we are negative, to register the awareness is something.

Observe how you behave in this room.

If we could relax small muscles and larger muscles as well, the negative states could not continue. Consider jealousy, the child is jealous, it does not want another child to approach its mother. It makes the movements we call jealousy, but the child's jealousy passes with the situation. Jealousy as a *Negative Emotion* persists long after the occasion which gave rise to it.

What is called intuition or telepathy is largely a matter of observation of *Moving Centre*. My dog always knows when I am depressed, or angry, why? Because when I am in those states I have those movements. (It may be smell, our states may change our smell). We are negative because we come early into contact with people who have many *Negative Emotions*, they have them without knowing it.

We are anxious about our jobs, our work; if we are doing our work from fear our centre of gravity is outside us. If we are identified when we are eating a beefsteak and are very angry when someone takes it away, we are that beefsteak. When the centre of gravity is within and all three centres are at work, that is absorption, and not identifying, and one can be aware of oneself without observation.

The theory of evolution is the most imbecile idea that ever hypnotised humanity, how could the greater grow out of less? Mankind, this body, this mind?

No amount of ordinary knowledge will change *Being*.

> There are seven kinds of man:
> 7
> 6
> 5 Conscious
> 4 Balanced
> 3 Intellectual
> 2 Emotional
> 1 Moving

Ordinarily we think of knowledge as something we can get at the university, but if I studied Chinese, medicine etc., I would still be the same. There are two circles of humanity, *mechanical and conscious*. There is knowledge belonging to conscious man, and knowledge belonging to mechanical man.

We think of man slowly evolving by changing a little here and a little there, of language as evolving. Somebody said 'Ba', then a hundred years later somebody else said 'Ba Ba'. This is imbecile. All culture was originated by *conscious man*, the *knowledge of conscious man* is always the same.

An analogy can be made with the body, the soft cells and the nervous system: the nervous system is protected and separated, the injuries to soft cells can be healed, the body cells live and die in 24 hours. An injury to the nervous system is irreparable, it never seems worth while patching it up.

Shock from new knowledge is at first conscious shock; the knowledge of Christ directly influenced his followers, but it is doubtful if we receive any force from Christ's Teaching today.

This shock cannot be continuous, how could it be ? To begin with, why should *conscious man* sacrifice himself by giving all this force to humanity, and does humanity want to be changed? Ask yourself that question and answer it.

Coercion is useless, we might make an order that everyone should change *Being* by next Saturday, or they would be beheaded. It would be useless, they might pretend to have changed. The wish to change must come from within. There is a phrase in the Work: we love our Negative Emotions.

If we could only *Self-Remember*, the results would be **miraculous**, but it is useless to say "I wish to *Self-Remember*," mechanically, it must be **emotional**. It is useless to remember every word I say. You may go on saying forever; "Yes *the world is asleep*". Of course the world is asleep, don't you know that the world is asleep? Unless you realise that you yourself are *asleep*, it is quite useless.

Pity and sympathy are not necessarily *Negative Emotions*. They can spring from understanding of someone's needs, from *External Considering*. They may come from understanding someone's difficulties in *The Work*. You might help by saying something, or more often by not saying anything. The person setting out to help us, and setting down with bag and baggage is not doing any good at all, and we resent it for a very good reason.

Conscious man must be replenished, but we could not teach a savage coming into this room, he must first be taught how to behave. It is necessary to be ordinarily educated and to have ordinary decent feelings, to come into *The Work*. The wish comes from possessing right *Magnetic Centre*. We might observe two kinds of literature and wonder why there are two kinds. This work is largely going against mechanical habits.

Have you *observed* how you can be in little 'I's and in bigger 'I's?

Emotional man, artist, *Emotional Centre* appreciates nature and art.

This *Work* is all *remembering*, if we could remember what we were yesterday and compare it with what we are today.

We can only imitate movement, expression, not thought. I cannot observe your thought, I don't know how you think, I can only observe and imitate the expression of it.

We don't know how we think, perhaps that is a mercy.

MAN AS A THREE STOREY HOUSE

Intellectual Centre	Higher Intellectual Centre
Emotional Centre	Higher Emotional Centre

Moving Centre	Instinctive Centre	Sex Centre

March 15, 1934

Maurice Nicoll: Nothing is "written" on *Intellectual* or *Emotional Centre*.

Something is "written" on *Instinctive Centre* or else the child could not suckle.

This *Work* teaches that *impressions* are most important. We do not take in *impressions* – we have no real sense of I. *Impressions* fall on *Personality*, if they fell on *Essence* they could pass on to H 24.

I remember hearing this question at the beginning when we were all in a very great muddle. What would happen if *impressions* fell on *Essence*? And the answer was given, and I think it was a very good answer: Everything would be more real. Can you distinguish yet when *impressions* have fallen on *Essence*? When I have been ill and Nicoll is more passive, I have looked at the bedroom and seen the pictures for the first time. We do not take in *impressions*; how many of you know the colour of the curtains in this room – perhaps the women do, I am sure the men don't.

We could take in more *impressions* now if we looked at what we saw, but we need more knowledge of how to take in *impressions*. We take in just enough to get along with, for the purposes of recognition, but we don't see the person we are most intimate with.

Savages are *Essence*, but they have only superstitions. *Essence* can only grow through the dissolution of *Personality*. The first stage is disillusion.

We don't take in impressions because we are preoccupied with ourselves; our preoccupation with our own miseries and our own unhappiness are quite useless.

We interfere with one another's lives, but we don't really want to help one another.

We learn to take in *impressions* by stopping *Internal Considering*, day-dreaming etc.

This *Work* goes in little steps, we must not try to do what is beyond us, what we are not strong enough for. I cannot do this, and this and this, but perhaps I can do this little thing. To try to do what is beyond us makes us pessimistic and negative.

Imagination can help us in this way. If we can see where we behave badly and could form a clear image of how we would like to behave, direct the imagination by the intellect, that might help us.

Ordinarily *imagination* is in control of us.

Miss X: Is man's position in the universe by analogy like that of a cell in the body that is not functioning properly?

Maurice Nicoll: No. you can't say that.

Man is made up of cells, is he not? Imagine seeing a piece of a body, somebody else's body, under a microscope. There are different kinds of cells which probably know nothing of one another. It is difficult to believe that they make up a man. Man should be either a brain cell or a sex cell, by analogy. There are different kinds of brain cells. Some are much more *mechanical* than others

Mrs.X: What happens to the man who is always mechanical?

Maurice Nicoll: I don't know what happens to him.

Man is an acorn, he can grow. He may become just a larger acorn, that is, not growing, or he may become a tree. Acorns are eaten by pigs. There are very unpleasant ways of being eaten. If you do not try to grow, you are just tossed to and fro by life. Because you are happy now that does not mean that you will be happy next week, or always. You won't. Life presents us with the most shattering experiences which we must be shielded against. Everything in life goes by opposites. Life gives, and then takes away. We must use life for our own purposes, then it has some significance. Otherwise it is just meaningless. We must use life, and be good at our jobs.

Heredity gives us the shape of our bodies, but not our *Essence*. *Essence* goes about seeking a body. Essence is from somewhere higher in the scale. Unless we change *essence* it will always in *recurrence* find the same parents and attract the same difficulties. We think we can change our circumstances, but we can only change them by changing our *Being*. *It is our Being that attracts those circumstances.*

Self-Remembering, this most important idea, *self-remembering* gives us the *First Conscious Shock*.

This *Work* is not theoretical. It is no use saying "I understand the theory of *Self-Remembering*."

Our 'I's are formed by imitation of father, mother, nurse, brothers, sisters, teachers, films, reading. Then we begin to pretend. All nature is dressed up and we dress up. The bird with ruffling plumage is dressed up because it is afraid.

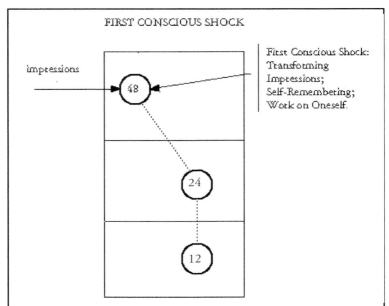

First Conscious Shock. This happens where Do 48 enters the upper storey of the "factory," where Hydrogen Mi 48 is present (from the beginning of the air octave.)

Identifying.

All envying is *Identifying*, all worrying is *Identifying*, all desire to score off another person is *Identifying*; one could go on all night.

To see a motor car and to want it is not *Identifying* yet, but to want it so much that you cannot think about this *Work*, or eat, or sleep, then your centre of gravity is completely outside you, and that is *Identifying*. We must find out how we *Identify* by observing recurrent situations over and over again.

After a while we get the taste of *Identifying*.

Heredity.

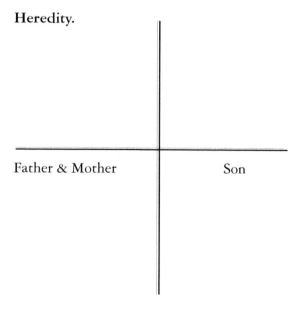

Father & Mother   Son

Being comes in on the vertical line, Being of son has always been there.

There are two kinds of knowledge:

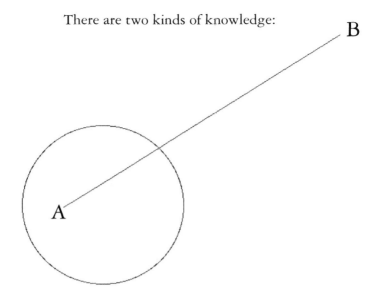

B Knowledge comes from outside, from *Greater Mind*, and is in life, in some literature (*New Testament*), in some art, and probably in some music.

A knowledge is also important, it is nice to have electric light, otherwise we would go about striking matches, we wouldn't even have the matches. We can't walk without boots. But all the *A knowledge* in the world would not change me.

Magnetic Centre in us realises that there is a difference in *B knowledge*, that it is on a different plane. Children ought to be brought up to know the difference. If they were brought up amongst machines, entirely, they would become sexless and sterile (literally).

There is nothing too bad that can be said about any of us, but we may be able to express a *negative emotion* less unpleasantly, or we may avoid some person in particular, because if we see them we will blow up.

Life is not this table, this static furniture, it is events, events all the time in this room, another event when you get outside into the street, another event when you receive a letter and begin rushing about; events are not in three dimensions.

Don't *identify* in the obvious ways, rushing to see an accident, getting into crowds (this is very bad for us). We identify when we read about things in the newspapers, that is an event.

We must go against our habits, habits of *identifying* in particular ways. Accurate *observation of oneself* is necessary.

There is definite Western Esotericism. It is not much use going to the East as what is easy for them to understand is very difficult for us.

Some people mix everything up, put everything on the same scale (*New Testament* and the *Sporting Times*), they revolt one. We cannot understand the *New Testament* now, only after many years we may begin to understand it.

Self suggestion is in the form "I will be a good man this week". This is too vague, it is useless. Imagination directed by intellect must be based on accurate observation.

Maurice Nicoll

March 22, 1934

Question: What is non-considering?

Maurice Nicoll: There are two forms of *considering*, *internal* and *external*. Internal is bad, external good. Non-considering is the stopping of *Internal Considering*. *Internal Considering* is having accounts with people, what they owe us, not what we owe them or how we can pay them back for their injuries. It is also always thinking about what other people are thinking, have thought, will think about us. Being pleased if they are pleased with us, unhappy if they are cross; unhappy if we are not dressed properly. It is very difficult to define, it is not quite any of these things. People may become ill through *Inner-Considering*, some do it a great deal more than others.

External Considering is good, it is putting yourself in the other's place. This requires effort and does not come from *Moving Centre*. *Internal Considering* requires no effort (except to stop it) and it is mechanical.

External and *Internal Considering* are always applied to people, not to things. I cannot *Externally Consider* this table. Sometimes it is amusing when we hit our foot and curse the door, trying to *Internally Consider* it. We identify with things, we do not internally consider them.

Internal Considering takes a great deal of force from us. We are subnormal and must try to grow normal.

Internal Considering is connected with *Negative Emotions*. We have to *observe ourselves* to realise how many *Negative Emotions* we have. We often don't realise them as such until we observe ourselves.

Thinking? Talking? Most of our talking is just scandal, polite and less polite. This takes force and we must try to stop it. We must try to stop *Internal considering* and *Negative Emotions* from some definite aim in *The Work*. E.g. scandal takes force from us. *Lying* destroys *Essence*. *Lying* means all forms of pretence as well as actual lies.

Mr.X: Do we observe ourselves with a special 'I'?

Maurice Nicoll: With *Self-Observing 'I'*; this is good enough for practical purposes.

Usually we do not remember our 'I's. We pass from one to another without noticing, although other people may notice through our expression or intonation. This is because all our 'I's use one mouth, therefore we think they are the same person. People who have been in The Work for two or three years will realise how few of their 'I's have heard of this Work. *Self-Observation* forms a bridge between these 'I's.

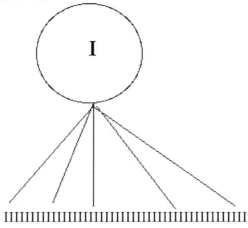

We connect that 'I' we were in five minutes ago with the one we are in now and gradually a bridge linking them grows up. These 'I's may grow and form a group of 'I's round *Observing 'I'*.

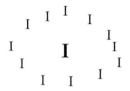

This is called *Deputy Steward*. We have to aim at this stage.

Stages: *Master*
          Steward
          Deputy Steward
          Observing I

The Master comes when we have complete knowledge of all the 'I's of and in our whole life.

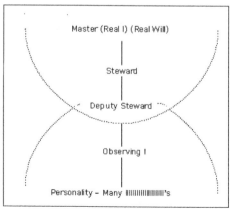

**DR.NICOLL'S FIRST INSTRUCTIONS
TO HIS GROUP IN 1931**

Remember Yourself
Observe Yourself
Do not Internally Consider
Do not Identify
Do not express Negative Emotions
Struggle with Imagination

April 12, 1934

Question: How can we step out of our associations with particular people?

Maurice Nicoll: These associations are our limited round, our orbit of *sleep*. First of all we must realise that we don't know people. All *The Work* is about this.

Organic life is created for two purposes. One might start a business for two reasons; to help oneself or to help other people. If it did not help oneself at all one would give up. *Organic life* can ascend or descend; but some must ascend or this little bit of the universe, earth and moon, will be cut off and will not be missed in the universe. It is very important to think of this, that this is a *growing universe*, and the sun demands that some should grow.

The three notes of the *octave* are explained simply as constituting *organic life*. In the old myths the heroes are solar heroes.

It is necessary to work in the big plan.

In the New Testament passages are connected which we do not usually think of as being connected.

St.Luke xiii:

There were present at that season some that told Him of the Galileans, whose blood Pilate had mingled with their sacrifices.

And Jesus answering said to them, 'Suppose ye that these Galileans were sinners above all Galileans, because they suffered such things?

I tell you nay: but, except ye repent, ye shall all likewise perish.

Or those eighteen, upon whom the tower in Siloam

fell, and slew them, think ye that they were sinners above all men that dwelt in Jerusalem?

I tell you, Nay: but, except ye repent, ye shall all likewise perish.

He spake also this parable: 'A certain man had a fig tree planted in his vineyard; and he came and sought fruit thereon, and found none.

The he said unto the dresser of his vineyard; 'Behold, these three years I come seeking fruit on this fig tree, and find none: cut it down; why cumbereth it the ground?'

And he answering Him said; 'Lord, let it alone this year also, till I dig about it, and dung it.'

And if it bear fruit, well; and if not, then after that thou shalt cut it down.

These three are connected. In the first two the disciples are not told to draw conclusions from what they see in life, *life is under the Law of Accident*. It is necessary to grow and to come under other laws, the *Law of Fate*, or the same things will happen to them, they will be under the *Law of Accident*. To repent means to take another view of things, not the materialistic view – to have another *Neutralising Force*.

Because we are under the *Law of Accident* many of you are in circumstances which have nothing to do with what you are essentially; and even after you have come into contact with this *Work* the same things go on, lunches, dinners, etc. We must drop people who only complicate our lives.

When we get into certain negative states we believe that those states are permanent. It is like looking out of one window of a house and in a sense what we see is true but we forget that there are other windows. We must get to the point of finding our moods wearisome.

We are like a citadel in which there are 'I's connected with *The Work* (intelligentsia); and some very bad 'I's which immediatly want to damage *The Work* and which must be taught. We cannot remember our *aim* for five seconds.

We should *observe ourselves* like making photographs of ourselves and putting them in an album, without criticism; because we criticise from the ordinary point of view, which we are doing all the time. We should begin by observing how we move, and where we are; usually we are not aware of this.

We cannot *Externally Consider*. Briefly, *External Considering* is **doing the right thing at the right time**, but we cannot do this. We can only do this if we are *Self-Remembering*, and we do not *Self-Remember*. We should not *Internally Consider*; not bother about what people are thinking of us. Some people do not feel right if they have not the right tie on; everything is then artificial: there is no sense of 'I' at all.

In the group *Internal Considering* stops the questions, makes everything dead.

Consciousness has nothing to do with evolution in the ordinary sense. There has always been consciousness; perhaps more in the time of Christ than at any other time; the difficulties were greater then. You had to be prepared to give up your life. Now everything is too easy for us. One cannot make difficulties, difficulties come up if one begins to work. Find someone of whom you disapprove and try to be that person. If you are a violent Tory, try to take the other point of view, just for exercise. One should go against one's *mechanicalness*. If one does not think much, it is difficult to begin to think; if one does not move much, it is difficult to move; if one does not feel much, it is difficult to begin to feel. It is our *mechanicalness* that makes us act in the way we do, not because we are under the *Law of Accident*.

Identifying makes us tired; paying attention gives us force. At a football match, if one shouts and identifies it does not stay with one. If one pays attention and tries to see why some particular player always makes the same mistake it stays with one. Life takes our force because we *Identify*.

Self-Justification is not *Internally Considering*. It touches it. All these things touch each other, but they are not the same.

Internal Considering is not the opposite of *External Considering*. It is *keeping accounts*.

April 21, 1934

Maurice Nicoll: There was much force in the time of Christ. Perhaps it was an important crisis. The *Conscious Circle of Humanity* gives these shocks at certain times in history. There were many *Schools* at that time apart from Christ, if Christ existed. There was a great deal of force left lying about for anybody who could pick it up; for those who had ears to hear.

Question: Did living in the fear of death give more force?

Maurice Nicoll: This system is not invented by some clever man; it comes from somewhere much higher up. It gives us a key to *Greater Mind*. It is a lever by which you can raise your *level of Being*. We are in what is called ordinary waking state. By *Self-Observation* we can raise our *level of Being* just a little.

——————————————————————— Self-Remembering

Result of Self-Remembering

Ordinary Waking State

We may observe our ordinary level of talking, how *mechanical* it is, and if we begin to dislike the way we talk we may stop talking like that. If we were *observing ourselves* when certain *impressions* are presented to us, we might get something from them, if we are not they are just wasted.

71

Miss X: Is *Self-Observation*, *Self-Remembering*, connected with the saying "The Kingdom of God is within you"?

Maurice Nicoll: Yes, everything is within you. It is no use going somewhere else to look for it. The idea of the Kingdom of Heaven comes up in literature, for example Francis Bacon.

There are *three kinds of mechanical man*. They are not more important than one another, one kind is not superior to another. They all go to make up the big man, *Organic Life*.

The first kind of man is the most common. *Moving* or *Instinctive* man thinks like this: 'Will I have a comfortable bed? If not, I won't go'. The second kind of man, artistic man (not necessarily an artist), is *emotional.* The third kind of man is the *intellectual* man. Darwin finished up by being intellectual anyhow. You should try to put people into these categories: 3-2-1, 3-1-2, 2-3-1, 2-1-3, 1-3-2, 1-2-3. There is Christianity for three kinds of man; for *Moving* type man Christianity is ritual, colour etc.

We only know different degrees of *Negative Emotion.* What we think are our positive emotions belong to emotional part of *Moving Centre*.

We have no business to be saying 'I like' or 'I dislike'. We do not know enough about anybody to say we like or dislike them.

One must evade questions, otherwise one has to uphold one's position, one must always like and dislike what one has said one likes and dislikes. We hear people on buses; 'Do you like?' and 'Do you dislike?' and getting wildly excited. After a while in *The Work* one does not want to feel like this. One does not want to get excited about films and murder stories. One must observe *lying* not only in oneself but in life and in the newspapers.

We should try to stop thinking, even if for only five seconds a day, get out of the round. At first just try to stop, and find that you cannot, if you stop thought in one place it comes up in another. Then try fixing your *attention* on an image of something. Thinking about this Work, *Self-Remembering* for instance, is something quite different. By trying to think what *Self-Remembering* means for instance, one may get flashes of insight.

The words used, *Identifying* etc, are not capable of exact definition, they stand for something very great behind. We must struggle against *imagination*, *Identifying*, etc.

Chief Feature comes up not in big things but in little things. In big things we usually behave quite well, if there is a war for instance, we give our lives. It is in little things that we behave so badly.

People who come to this *Work* from curiosity or for amusement, who have not right *Magnetic Centre*, are sooner or later thrown out by *The Work*. *The Work* chooses its own.

There are fewer and fewer people with right *Magnetic Centre*. If no people had right *Magnetic Centre* we should become like ants. Consider Russia for instance. After listening to this Teaching for some time, one must ask oneself questions: Is this the key for me? What is my life? Can I manage it by myself?

Mechanical man, the self-sacrificing or the industrious man and the lazy person are both in the same position.

We are not balanced because of the wrong working of *Centres*. Our aim is to become balanced. It is a step towards *conscious man*.

People sometimes say that there is nothing about this in the New Testament, but take "Awake and pray" for example; we cannot pray unless we are awake.

Self-Remembering is mentioned in the diagram only in connection with *Intellectual Centre*, but there is *Self-Remembering* in all the Centres. If *impressions* pass on to H12, it alters the chemistry of the body.

Have you noticed violence in yourselves? *Negative Emotion* causes violence. It is because of planetary tension that there are wars. But if man were awake planetary tension would not have this effect. The tension causes other upheavals, earthquakes etc.

If you decide this *Work* is important to you, you must be prepared for many unpleasant times, because it goes in waves.

April 28, 1934

Maurice Nicoll: This *Work* is in parables because there is nothing in our ordinary consciousness that could understand it. If that were not so there would be no need for work or change. It speaks of something that ordinarily we do not understand. Take it on this level: if you want to bring anybody into this *Work* how would you explain it to them? What is there to go on? It is best not to talk too much about parables; the parable of the vineyard, the parable of the talents. Think of the two together. Get rid of the idea of money connected with talents. All people who come into this *Work* are paid alike, those who have been in a short time and those who have been in a long time. What you make of it is your concern. Those who have been in a long time are treated much more harshly as it were if they break rules or make a mistake.

Ordinarily our sense of ourselves is from pictures of ourselves and from possessions. Have you noticed pictures of yourselves? A picture of oneself as just, as always calm, as Good Samaritan (though that perhaps is more a role). If we receive a blow directly on a picture of ourselves we react very strongly. If we were more *awake* we could make use of it but the 'I's connected with the picture call in other 'I's which don't really belong to it as a kind of police to protect the picture, although not everybody reacts like that. We don't need to think to act from a picture, it is mechanical. We must separate ourselves from this mechanicalness.

Chief Feature is like the axle of a wheel to which everything else belongs. If we could melt the axle as it were, everything else that was *mechanical* would disappear. It is like the beam of a house, if the beam were broken, the whole house would fall down.

We cannot be shown *Chief Feature* before we are ready for it, or the house would fall and there would be nothing left, we would go mad. Our ordinary reaction when we are told our *Chief Feature* is to laugh at it. "Oh, that!" And then the tendency is to show *Chief Feature* more than ever for a time. Then after 3 or 4 years we begin to become uncomfortable about it. If we worked only on *Chief Feature* everything else would disappear or begin to, so I was told. It is easier to see someone else's *Chief Feature* than one's own.

Nothing prevents *impressions* falling on *Essence* as much as *lying*, lying of that sort, pictures, imagination. *Imagination* is very real and very strong. The lies form a network which catches the *impressions* so that they cannot fall upon *Essence*, so that things are not as bright as they should be. We should really be in a state of *Self-Remembering* but we have fallen from it. If we were *Self-Remembering* we could not be unbalanced, or *mechanical*. It is because we do not *Self-Remember* that there is wrong working of *Centres*.

There are three kinds of *imagination*: that which does not speak, that which speaks but does not act, and that which acts.

Try not to express your *Negative Emotions*. Or anyhow try not to express them so unpleasantly, and do not write letters when you are feeling negative. This is a piece of practical advice. Don't write when you are full of *self-pity* for instance. You may want to write a letter, and you may think that you are in this *Work* and must not write this letter. But you say "Oh yes, this letter must be written, I will just scratch out a line."

Observe some particular way of being negative in yourselves and struggle against this. Don't think, "Oh this is unimportant, I will wait for something bigger".

People should not be frightened when they begin to change. It could only be to something better, it could not be worse.

It is better to think one is nothing; things go wrong if one thinks one is something.

Chief Feature is four dimensional, in time. Words are three dimensional. It is very difficult to express *Chief Feature* in words for that reason.

If you establish a place of light, mysterious things begin to happen. Personality begins to weaken, one begins to be a little uncomfortable. One passes through the outer layers one has taken oneself for. I have to observe my vanity, my depression, doubting side. Not simply identify with them. These things become more objective, and I pass a knife under them. This is done very slowly. This is why organisation is necessary. Self evolution can only be done by gradual understanding.

Combining Good and Truth now
by Bob Hunter
Dr Maurice Nicoll (1884-1953)

Maurice Nicoll's special contribution to the Fourth Way is that his teaching, by leavening the method transmitted by P.D. Ouspensky, helps people to value The Work. Where Ouspensky presented truth precisely, Nicoll in a more relaxed manner showed how to see the good of it. For truth has meaning only when it is made part of one's understanding; that is, when it combines with the good, which includes its reason and 'end'. Emphasising Good's precedence over Truth, Nicoll maintained that if we were good we would not need truth.

In his Gospel studies, he equated the name Christ with Truth and Jesus with Good; and hinted at the significance; in the united term's appearing only twice in the *New Testament*. Nicoll's full acceptance of Gurdjieff's assertion that The Work is Esoteric Christianity does not suggest he was to any degree sactimonious. On the contrary, he warned that anyone who affected a serious mien to appear to be a follower of the Fourth Way probably was far from it. He had a light touch, with people and in his writing, an approach partly explained by the Platonic saying artistically inscribed on a wall at one of his group houses: "Serious things can be understood through laughable things."

This inner lightness ruled out any thought of compulsion in his teaching, as shown for instance by his care never to say that people have no right to indulge in negative emotions, pointing out instead that they *have a right not to be negative*. Purification of the emotional centre was one of the main thrusts of Nicoll's teaching. He constantly illustrated ways in which negative emotions close the door to higher centres, which in turn hold the key to self-development.

Students accustomed to the rather rarified atmosphere of Work meeting rooms in the 'thirties and 'forties were at first startled to find Dr Nicoll holding court in a village pub. Not everyone realised how much of their False Personality they revealed at these convivial occasions, although most eventually observed that their teacher was always 'present' and that a casual remark might show them much about an attitude they were displaying.

Dr Nicoll could be starkly frank when circumstances demanded and his down-to-earth way of illustrating a message made it memorable. Such an occasion was when he drove home the idea that each essence is unique by telling a woman that, though she hoped to blossom into a rose, she was meant to grow into a blooming great poppy. At another time he had people rush about in a crowded room while carrying chairs with the legs sticking out. The resultant collisions etched in the mind the way that jagged points of our False Personalities catch against those of other people, for we see only the outer person instead of allowing for inner qualities.

He continually used this ability to evoke striking

images to teach The Work. One of his suggestions was that people draw a map of their psychological country, to know where it was safe to move about interiorly. To help people separate from useless self-blame for wrong thinking, he described thoughts as birds and said people were responsible for them only if they trapped them in the birdcage of their minds, instead of letting them fly away.

Most people in The Work know of Nicoll through the energising thoughts expressed in his books. Henry Maurice Dunlop Nicoll, was born in Kelso, Scotland, in 1884, the son of a Free Church minister, the Rev William Robertson Nicoll (later Sir William, after ill health forced him to give up the ministry, which led to his becoming a leading man of letters). Maurice spent his boyhood in Hampstead, London, took a first in Science at Caius College, Cambridge, qualified in medicine at Bart's Hospital, studied psychology under Freud then Jung and became a leading Harley Street consultant. He was a captain in the RAMC in World War I, being in charge of a hospital in Gallipoli, an experience described in his book *In Mesopotamia* in 1917, in which year he also published *Dream Psychology*.

He had a fulfilling career, but his life's aim changed when he heard Ouspensky lecture in London in 1921; and after hearing Gurdjieff the next year he relinquished his medical consultancy and, accompanied by his wife, Catherine, and their baby daughter, joined the *Institute for the Harmonious Development of Man* in France. When, a year later, Gurdjieff indicated the Institute was closing, the Nicolls returned to Ouspensky's group. Ouspensky's centre of gravity may have seemed to be his intellect, but with Nicoll he gave more expression to his feelings. It was said that Nicoll was only person in the group who could make the master laugh, and he sometimes stayed with the Nicoll family at their country cottage. Despite this compatibility, in 1931 Ouspensky said, according to his pupil: "Nicoll, you had better go away... Go away, and teach the system."

This he did for the rest of his life, supported by Mrs Nicoll in a relationship that may well have inspired his comment: "A real marriage is when two people are working. It can be in essence. When he is asleep she must be awake. When she is asleep he must be awake."

Dr Nicoll's most influential written works were not intended for publication, which he greeted with 'humble amazement'. The first volume of his invaluable *Psychological Commentaries on the Teaching of G.I. Gurdjieff and P.D. Ouspensky*, a collection of papers read to his groups; was printed as a matter of some urgency after he confided to senior pupils in 1948 that he would not live much longer and that Catherine should carry on The Work teaching. He survived long enough, however, to see three volumes in print; volume four and five were editied by his secretary, Beryl Pogson.

Volume One had been printed in 1949, the year when Gurdjieff announced it was time for the esoteric teaching to become more widely known. Publisher Vincent Stuart, one of Nicoll's pupils suggested he also produce a book from the "Gospels chapters" and this appeared in 1950 as *The New Man*.

Vincent Stuart brought out Nicoll's classic *Living Time* in 1952. It had been written 23 years earlier, when publication of ideas relating to the Work system was banned. However, Beryl Pogson reveals in her biography *Maurice Nicoll; A Portrait*, by collecting "all the thoughts about Time and Eternity that had come to him from Hermetic literature, from the Greeks, the neo-Platonists, from the mystics throughout the ages, and from Ouspensky whose Theory of Recurrence was not part of Gurdjieff's system" he was able to present similar notions to a new audience.

It is natural that the idea of recurrence, bearing as it does on the 'whither' part of the vital question that confronts us all, should attract attention, and perhaps stir debate, among Nicoll's readers. He always made clear that identical recurrence was a mathematical idea of Ouspensky. As far as can be gleaned from his writing and from teaching in groups that follow his tradition, Nicoll accepted psychological recurrence as a reality and believed in what might be termed a form of reincarnation in which one's essence returns to visible life with the understanding it has made its own. Such spiritual persistence means that, even in physical recurrence, a person who has reached a higher level of being will be ready to relate to other people earlier than in previous existences.

This line of thought implies an eternal plan and an invisible guiding intelligence that assists the development of consciousness. Dr Nicoll spoke of the universe as "infinite response", adding for those of us who may not find it so that it "is intelligent in so far as we are intelligent". To live intelligently requires sustained effort, but he pointed out that "the response is more than that we furnish to produce this response".

In 1952 Dr Nicoll was still writing chapters for another book on the Gospels which was published posthumously as *The Mark*. He had previously told members of his group that the Greek word usually translated as 'sin' originally meant to miss the mark, and thus was free of guilt associations; on his birthday in July he added: "You cannot have an aim without a mark... the Mark is the Kingdom of Heaven." The heaven he meant is an inner state, a higher level, that can be attained now.

Writing (in *Living Time*) for a public not necessarily familiar with Work terms, Nicoll said that, were our potential of consciousness raised so we could dwell in the now, each moment would be registered and we would leave "a trace of ourselves".

Maurice Nicoll left more than a trace.

Note:

Details of Dr Nicoll's life are given in:

Maurice Nicoll: A Portrait by Beryl Pogson; Eureka Editions 2004 (first published 1961).

Maurice Nicoll, Portrait of a Vertical Man by Samuel Copley; Swayne Publications, London, 1989.

Dr Nicoll enjoying a beer in the public house 'George IV' while conversing with members of his group and local people.

photograph by Michael Rubinstein.

BIBLIOGRAPHY

GURDJIEFF, G.I. *Beelzebub's Tales to his Grandson* Routledge&Kegan Paul, 1950

Unaltered reprint by The Two Rivers Press, 1993 NICOLL, Maurice *Informal Work Talks and Teachings* Eureka Editions 2000

NICOLL, Maurice *Living Time* Eureka Editions 1998

NICOLL, Maurice *Psychological Commentaries on the Teaching of Gurdjieff and Ouspensky* Eureka Editions 2008, 6 vols with index.

NICOLL, Maurice *Simple Explanation of Work Ideas* Eureka Editions 1998.

NICOLL, Maurice *The Mark* Eureka Editions 1998

NICOLL, Maurice *The New Man* Eureka Editions 1998

POGSON, Beryl *Maurice Nicoll, A Portrait* Eureka Editions 2004

COPLEY, Sam *Portrait of a Vertical Man* "Maurice Nicoll, An Appreciation" Swayne Publications, 1989

OUSPENSKY,P.D. *In Search of the Miraculous* Routledge & Kegan Paul,1950

OUSPENSKY,P.D. *The Fourth Way* Routledge&Kegan Paul, 1967.

OUSPENSKY,P.D. *The Psychology of Man's Possible Evolution* Vintage Books, 1981

POGSON, Beryl *Commentary on the Fourth Gospel* Eureka Editions 2000

POGSON, Beryl *In the East my Pleasure lies and other esoteric interpretations of plays by William Shakespeare* Eureka Editions 1999

POGSON, Beryl *More Work Talks* Eureka Editions 2014

POGSON, Beryl *The Work Life* Eureka Editions 2014

POGSON, Beryl *Work Talks at the Dicker 1966* Eureka Editions 2012

POGSON, Beryl *Work Talks in Brighton* Eureka Editions 2014

(POGSON) *Centenary Fragments* by Beryl Pogson Eureka Editions 2008

(POGSON) *Practical Work Tasks* Eureka Editions, 2000, 55 pages.

(POGSON) *Unforgotten Fragments* Beryl Pogson and Others Eureka Editions 2007

INDEX

NOTES

NOTES

NOTES

NOTES

Printed in Great Britain
by Amazon